The Countries

The United States

Bob Italia

ABDO Publishing Company

visit us at
www.abdopub.com

Published by ABDO Publishing Company, 4940 Viking Drive, Edina, Minnesota 55435.
Copyright © 2003 by Abdo Consulting Group, Inc. International copyrights reserved in all countries. No part of this book may be reproduced in any form without written permission from the publisher.

Printed in the United States.

Photo Credits: Corbis
Contributing Editors: Tamara L. Britton, Kristin Van Cleaf, Stephanie Hedlund,
    Jennifer R. Krueger
Art Direction & Maps: Neil Klinepier

Library of Congress Cataloging-in-Publication Data

Italia, Bob, 1955-
    The United States / Bob Italia.
        p. cm. — (The countries)
    Includes index.
    Summary: An overview of the history, geography, plant and animal life, people, economy, cities, transportation and communication, government, sports and leisure, and holidays of the United States of America.
        ISBN 1-57765-845-0
        1. United States—Juvenile literature. [1. United States.] I. Title. II. Series.

E156 .I83 2002
973--dc21

                                                    2002020762

Contents

Hello!

Hello from the United States of America! The U.S. is the world's third-largest country in both population and area. Only China and India have more people. Only Russia and Canada have more land.

The U.S. is big and covers a large area. Because of this, the country has many different plants, animals, and climates.

Some countries have a long history, but the U.S. does not. In a short time, the country has become an **economic** and military power.

The U.S. has a **democratic** government. This offers its citizens many freedoms and opportunities. The U.S. has the world's most productive economy. So its people enjoy one of the world's highest standards of living.

The U.S. has great resources, a healthy **economy**, and a diverse population. These factors have helped the nation become the world leader that it is today.

Hello from the United States!

Fast Facts

OFFICIAL NAME: The United States of America
CAPITAL: Washington, D.C.

LAND
- Area: 3,717,810 square miles (9,629,091 sq km)
- Mountain Ranges: Rocky Mountains, Appalachian Mountains
- Highest Point: Mount McKinley 20,320 feet (6,194 m)
- Major Rivers: Mississippi, Colorado, Hudson, Missouri

PEOPLE
- Population: 278,058,881 (July 2001 est.)
- Major Cities: New York City, Los Angeles, Chicago, Washington, D.C.
- Languages: English, Spanish
- Religions: Protestantism, Catholicism, Judaism, Islam

GOVERNMENT
- Form: Federal republic
- Head of Government: President
- Legislature: Congress
- National Anthem: "The Star-Spangled Banner"
- Flag: Thirteen horizontal stripes, alternating between red and white. A blue field on the upper mast side contains 50 stars, one for each state.
- Independence: July 4, 1776

ECONOMY
- Agricultural Products: Wheat, corn, fruit, vegetables, cotton; beef, pork, poultry, fish, dairy products; forestry products
- Mining Products: Petroleum, natural gas, coal
- Manufactured Products: Petroleum products, steel, cars, chemicals, electronics, processed foods, textiles, lumber
- Money: U.S. dollar (1 dollar = 100 cents)

Washington, D.C.

Alaska

Hawaii

The United States's Flag

A 100 dollar bill

Timeline

1600s	British explorers colonize east coast
1776	Colonies declare independence from Britain
1861-1865	Civil War
1917	U.S. enters World War I
1918	World War I ends
1929	Stock market crashes, Great Depression begins
1941	U.S. enters World War II
1945	U.S. drops atomic bombs on Japan; war ends
1950-1953	Korean War
1962	U.S. military advisers sent to Vietnam
1973	Vietnam War ends
1991	Persian Gulf War
2001	Terrorists crash planes into the World Trade Center, the Pentagon, and a Pennsylvania field

A Brief History

Before Europeans arrived, Native Americans lived on the land that would become the United States. In the early A.D. 1600s, British explorers started colonies along the eastern coast of North America.

Thomas Jefferson became the nation's third president.

The colonists and Native Americans fought over the land. But the colonists had better weapons and won many of the battles. Eventually, the Native Americans moved west.

Britain's King George III ruled the colonies. He charged the colonists heavy taxes. But the colonists did not think this was fair. They had no representation in Britain's government.

So Thomas Jefferson wrote the **Declaration of Independence**. In 1776, the colonies declared their independence.

George Washington

But King George did not want to give up the colonies. So the colonists and the British fought the **American Revolution**. The colonists won and formed the United States of America. In 1789, George Washington became the country's first president.

Soon Americans began settling the land to the west. Many Americans thought it was the nation's right to settle the continent from the Atlantic Ocean to the Pacific Ocean. They called this Manifest Destiny.

The Native Americans fought with the settlers over the land. But the Native Americans were outnumbered.

Abraham Lincoln

Eventually, Native Americans were moved to **reservations**. Americans then settled the country from coast to coast.

Soon, many new states joined the nation. But in 1861, 11 southern states withdrew from the **Union**. They wanted to form an independent nation. This started the **Civil War**.

In 1865, the Union won the war, and the U.S. remained united. But the next year, President Abraham Lincoln was **assassinated**. It was the first time a president was killed while in office.

By the 1900s, the U.S. was one of the world's strongest military powers. It defended **democracy** throughout the world by fighting in many wars.

The U.S. entered **World War I** in 1917. Under President Woodrow Wilson's leadership, the U.S. and its **allies** won the war the next year.

Woodrow Wilson

Throughout the 1920s, the nation's **economy** grew. But in 1929, the **stock market** crashed. This started the **Great Depression**. Many people lost their jobs. Soon this economic instability spread throughout the world.

Franklin D. Roosevelt was elected president in 1932. He created the **New Deal** to improve the nation's economy. The economy was struggling to improve when the nation was again called to war.

Franklin D. Roosevelt

The U.S. entered **World War II** in 1941. President Roosevelt died before the war was over.

In 1945, President Harry Truman made the historic decision to drop **atomic bombs** on Japan. Japan surrendered, and the U.S. and its **allies** won the war.

In 1950, President Truman sent Americans to help South Korea defend itself against North Korea in the **Korean War**. The two nations signed a **cease-fire** in 1953.

In 1962, President John F. Kennedy sent military advisers to Vietnam. The advisers went to help South Vietnam defend itself against North Vietnam in the **Vietnam War**. President Kennedy was **assassinated** in 1963.

The fighting in Vietnam worsened. In 1964, President Lyndon B. Johnson sent even more troops to fight in the war. Many Americans protested the war.

In 1968, Richard M. Nixon was elected president. He worked to end the war. But in 1972, a group of **Republicans** tried to steal information from the **Democrats**.

Nixon knew about the theft and tried to keep it a secret. Congress wanted to **impeach** him for lying. So Nixon resigned. The U.S. lost the **Vietnam War** in 1973.

In 1991, President George H. W. Bush led the U.S. during the **Persian Gulf War**. The

Richard M. Nixon

U.S. and its **allies** won the war. But the **economy** was weak. So in 1992, Americans elected Bill Clinton.

Americans were excited about their new president. He promised to improve the economy. Soon, new technology and the creation of Internet companies called dot-coms sparked the greatest economic boom since the **Industrial Revolution**.

Bill Clinton

But in 1998, President Clinton was accused of committing **perjury**. He was **impeached**. But at his trial, he was found not guilty. So he remained in office.

In 2000, the people elected George W. Bush. On
September 11, 2001, **terrorists** flew airplanes into the
World Trade Center and the Pentagon. Terrorists
crashed another plane in a Pennsylvania field.

President Bush led the nation in the **War on
Terrorism**. But the terrorist attacks disrupted the
economy. Many dot-coms also failed,
worsening the economy further.

Today, the U.S. continues to fight
terrorism around the world.
Americans are working to improve
the economy. And the nation
continues to be a world leader in
industry, economics, and defense.

George W. Bush

The Land

The United States is a large country that covers a vast area. So scientists have divided the land into seven regions. They are the Appalachian Highlands, the Atlantic Coastal Plain, the Central Lowland, the Great Plains, the Rocky Mountain Region, the Western **Intermontane** Region, and the Pacific Coastal Ranges.

The Appalachian Highlands extends from Maine to Alabama. This region has many mountain ranges.

The Atlantic Coastal Plain begins in Massachusetts and stretches south to Texas. Its rivers, beaches, bays, and offshore islands make it a popular vacation area.

West of the Appalachian Highlands is the Central Lowland. Its northern part has lakes and forests. Farther west is a large grassland called the Great Plains. Few trees grow there.

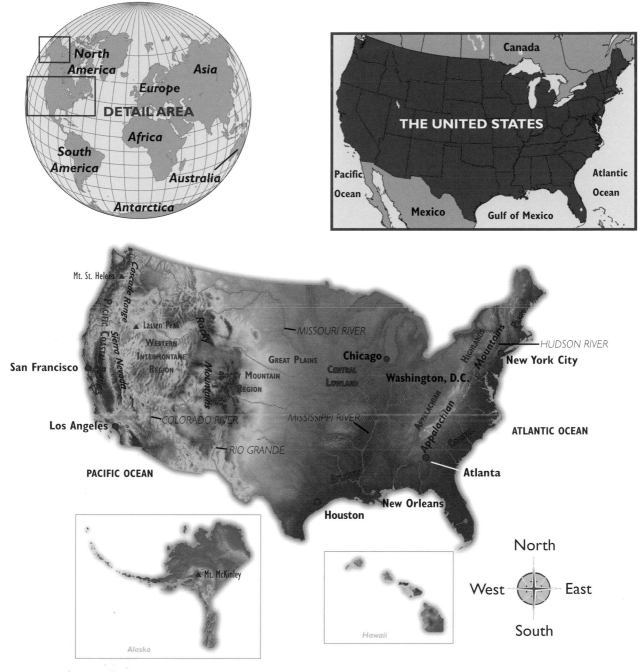

North America's largest mountain range is the Rocky Mountains. They stretch from northern Alaska to northern New Mexico. The Colorado River, the Missouri River, and the Rio Grande begin in the Rockies.

West of the Rocky Mountains lies the Western **Intermontane** Region. This region extends from

The Great Plains

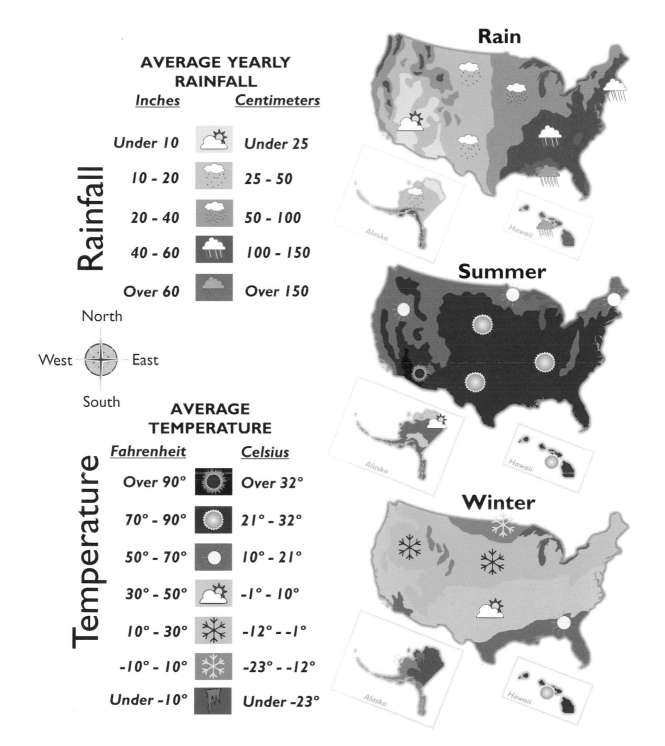

Washington to Mexico. Part of it is desert. But it also has forested mountains.

The Pacific Coastal Ranges region stretches from Washington through most of California. This region has two mountain ranges. They are the Cascade Range in the north, and the Sierra Nevada in the south.

The Cascade Range has two active volcanoes. They are Lassen Peak in California and Mount St. Helens in

The Rocky Mountains

A Hawaiian beach

Washington. Some of the range's highest peaks are covered by glaciers. Forests grow on the lower slopes.

The U.S. has a variety of climates throughout its land regions. The Midwest, the Middle Atlantic states, and New England have warm summers and cold, snowy winters. In the south, summers are long and hot, and winters are mild.

The western mountains are cooler and wetter than the plains and **plateaus**. Much of the west and southwest has a hot, dry, desert climate. Because of the ocean, the Pacific Coast's climate is mild all year.

Plants & Animals

The United States's varied land and climate make it rich in plant and animal life. Each region has distinctive plants and animals.

GENERAL SHERMAN

In the west, **coniferous** forests grow in the lower mountains and high **plateaus** of the Rocky Mountains, Cascade Range, and Sierra Nevada. Various kinds of pine, fir, and spruce grow there. Western hemlock, red cedar, and redwood trees grow there, too. The region's sequoia trees are world famous.

The General Sherman sequoia tree is the largest living thing on Earth.

From Maine to Minnesota, **coniferous** forests include pines, firs, and hemlock. Smaller forests of tamarack, spruce, paper birch, willow, alder, and aspen or poplar also grow there. Farther south, hardwood forests grow. Trees in these forests include oak, ash, walnut, and hickory.

On the Atlantic Coastal Plain, hickory, oak, magnolia, white cedar, and ash trees grow. Bald cypress, tupelo, and white cedar grow in swampy areas. This region also supports palmetto and oak trees.

In the Great Plains, grasslands extend westward to the Rocky Mountains. Many types of grasses grow there. They include buffalo, needle, and wheat grass.

The southwestern desert areas are dry. There, cactus, yucca, creosote bushes, and mesquite trees grow. A plant called the Joshua tree is also common.

Across these land regions, animal life is plentiful. Harbor and harp seals are found on both coasts. Sea lions live only along the Pacific Coast. Florida's large rivers are home to manatees. Manatees are often called sea cows.

The southwestern deserts are home to many poisonous reptiles, such as rattlesnakes and Gila monsters. Mammals in these areas include kangaroo rats, ring-tailed cats, and peccaries.

An American bison

Many animals, such as pikas and marmots, live in the western mountains. Rocky Mountain goats can be seen standing on sheer mountain sides!

The most famous grassland animals are American bison. They are often called buffalo. Pronghorn live in the grasslands, too. And prairie dogs and prairie chickens can only be found in North America.

White-tailed deer, black bears, gray foxes, raccoons, and opossums live in most of the nation's forests. Bald eagles, wild turkeys, woodpeckers, tanagers, American orioles, and hummingbirds fill the skies.

The Founding Fathers made the bald eagle the United States's national symbol in 1782.

Americans

The United States's people come from all over the world. The first people to live on the land were Native Americans, Alaska Natives, and Hawaiians.

Today's Native Americans and Alaska Natives are descendents of people from Asia. They **migrated** to North America about 35,000 years ago. The ancestors

An Alaska Native family

of today's Hawaiians **migrated** from French Polynesia. They arrived around A.D. 400.

Most white Americans are descended from European immigrants. Until the late 1800s, most of the immigrants came from northern and western Europe. Soon, others arrived from southern and eastern European nations.

Most Hispanic Americans are descendants of people from Spain, Mexico, Cuba, and Puerto Rico. Many African-Americans are descendants of Africans who came to the U.S. as slaves between the 1600s and 1800s. Later, people from many African nations immigrated to the U.S.

Since the 1800s, many immigrants have arrived from Asia. Most Asian Americans have ancestors from China, India, Vietnam, Japan, Korea, or the Philippines.

The U.S. does not have an official language, but most Americans speak English. Spanish is the second most common language.

The U.S. does not have an official religion. But many Americans are members of an organized religious group. Most are Protestant, Roman Catholic, Jewish, or Muslim.

Public education in the U.S. is free through high school. Most American children begin kindergarten around age five. They go on to elementary school, junior high, and high school. More than half of all high school graduates attend colleges or universities.

Americans must attend school until they are 16 years old.

Most Americans live in cities and suburbs. They often live in apartments, condominiums, or single-family houses. Poorer people live in small apartments and houses. Many of these homes are provided by the government.

Many Americans live in suburban homes such as this one.

Since Americans come from all over the world, they eat many different kinds of foods. Typical American meals consist of meats, potatoes, and vegetables. Pizza, spaghetti, and hamburgers are also popular. Immigrants have influenced American food by introducing new cooking methods and spices.

Americans often enjoy eating outside in their yards.

Oatmeal Fudge Cookies

This delicious, no-bake cookie is popular with adults and children!

- 1/2 cup milk
- 2 cups white sugar
- 3 tb cocoa powder
- 1/2 cup butter

- 3 tb peanut butter
- 3 cups rolled oats
- 1 tsp vanilla extract

In a large saucepan combine milk, sugar, cocoa powder, butter, and peanut butter. Bring to a boil over medium heat, stirring constantly. When the mixture comes to a full boil, stop stirring and boil for 1 and 1/2 minutes. Remove from heat and stir in oats and vanilla. Quickly drop mixture by teaspoonfuls onto waxed paper. Cool. Makes about 4 dozen cookies.

AN IMPORTANT NOTE TO THE CHEF: Always have an adult help with the preparation and cooking of food. Never use kitchen utensils or appliances without adult permission and supervision.

LANGUAGE

English	Spanish
Yes _____	Sí (SEE)
No _____	No (NOH)
Thank you _____	Gracias (GRAH-see-ahs)
Please _____	Por Favor (pohr-fah-VOHR)
Hello _____	Hola (OH-lah)
Good-bye _____	Adiós (ah-dee-OHS)

The Economy

The United States has the world's most productive **economy**. Its factories make a variety of goods, including steel, chemicals, cars, clothing, computers, and electronics.

The U.S. has a large supply of natural resources, including **petroleum**, natural gas, and coal. The U.S. ranks second, after Saudi Arabia, in petroleum production. It is second to Russia in producing natural gas, and second to China in coal mining.

The U.S. is a world leader in agriculture. Its farmers grow enough crops to feed Americans. There is also enough left over to provide about a third of the world's food exports.

The American fishing industry catches about a fifth of the world's seafood each year. Most of the fish are from the Atlantic and Pacific Oceans and the Gulf of Mexico.

The U.S. gets its energy from many sources. **Petroleum**, natural gas, and coal generate energy in homes and industry. Energy also comes from nuclear and **hydroelectric** plants.

A worker assembles a computer at the Dell factory.

Beautiful Cities

New York City is the United States's largest city. It is one of the world's important centers of business, **culture**, and trade. The city's ports manage much of the nation's imports and exports.

New York City is the country's cultural center. Most of the country's largest publishers are there. It is the nation's center for professional theater. New York City is also home to some of the nation's largest museums and art galleries.

Los Angeles is the country's second-largest city. Its port is one of the nation's busiest. It is the industrial, financial, and trade center of the western U.S. It is among the nation's leaders in airplane and aerospace equipment production. The city's film and television industry is world famous.

Chicago is the third-largest city. It is one of the world's leading industrial and transportation centers. The Chicago area manufactures more fabricated metals and food products than any other part of the country.

New York City

Moving & Communicating

Millions of miles of streets, roads, and highways crisscross the United States. Cars are the most common form of passenger transportation. In bigger cities, people ride buses and subways.

The U.S. has some of the world's busiest airports. The largest airports are in New York City, Los Angeles, Chicago, and Atlanta. Chicago's O'Hare International is the world's busiest airport.

Railroads carry about one-third of the nation's freight. Few Americans ride on trains. But Amtrak trains provide much of the country's passenger train service.

There are many major ports in the U.S. The ports at New York City, Los Angeles, and Houston are the busiest in the nation. San Francisco and New Orleans also have important ports.

Americans' love for the automobile has created the need for a vast system of roads.

The U.S. has thousands of newspapers and radio stations. Most Americans also have a television, and many subscribe to cable television. There are hundreds of stations to choose from.

The Internet has also become an important part of the country's communications network. And many Americans use cellular phones.

Government

The United States is a federal **republic**. It is also a **democracy**. Its citizens elect the president, members of Congress, and other government officials to represent them. Citizens 18 and older may vote.

The U.S. **Constitution** created three separate branches of government. They are the legislative, executive, and judicial branches. Each branch has power over the others. This is called checks and balances.

The legislative branch consists of a two-house Congress. It is divided into the Senate and the House of Representatives. Congress creates, abolishes, and changes federal laws.

The president heads the executive branch. The executive branch enforces federal laws.

The judicial branch is made up of a system of federal courts and judges. It interprets the nation's laws. The Supreme Court is the highest court in the nation.

Washington, D.C., is the capital of the U.S. and the center of the federal government. Every year, millions of tourists visit the city's government buildings, monuments, and museums.

Opposite page: The United States Capitol building is in Washington, D.C. Its construction began in 1793. President George Washington laid the building's cornerstone.

Holidays

In the United States, there are no official national holidays. Congress and the president may establish legal holidays for federal employees. Each state decides which holidays it will observe.

New Year's Day is on January 1. But it is often celebrated the night before at New Year's Eve parties. Americans stay awake until midnight to welcome the new year.

Memorial Day is on the last Monday in May. It honors all Americans who have died in wars. On July 4, the nation celebrates the signing of the **Declaration of Independence**. Americans celebrate Independence Day with fireworks, picnics, and parades.

Labor Day is the first Monday in September. It is a day of rest for the country's workers. Thanksgiving Day is on the fourth Thursday in November. Families gather for a meal and remember what they are thankful for.

Christmas falls on December 25. Many Americans decorate with Christmas trees and lights. Family members and friends exchange gifts. Many people attend church services.

Americans also observe other holidays. People of different religions celebrate their religions' holidays. Important Americans are often honored on their birthday.

A respected family elder often carves a turkey at the Thanksgiving Day meal.

American Culture

The United States is a young country. But its diverse population, freedom, and **economy** have created a rich **culture**.

Millions of Americans enjoy watching professional sporting events. The most popular are car racing, baseball, basketball, and football. Many Americans also participate in amateur sports.

Many American children play soccer.

Many people enjoy motion pictures, plays, concerts, operas, and dance performances.

Americans also like to visit museums. Some famous museums are the Metropolitan Museum of Art in New York City, the Museum of Science and Industry in Chicago, and the Smithsonian Institution in Washington, D.C.

Mark Twain's real name was Samuel Clemens.

In the early 1800s, American authors began producing important literary works. Early writers include Washington Irving and James Fenimore Cooper. Louisa May Alcott, Mark Twain, William Faulkner, and Ernest Hemingway are other important American novelists.

Many famous painters have come from the U.S. John Singleton Copley, Winslow Homer, Georgia O'Keeffe, and Andrew Wyeth are popular American painters.

American architects have designed buildings that have had a big impact on **architecture**. Frank Lloyd Wright was one of the nation's most imaginative architects.

In the early 1900s, motion pictures became an important art form. Americans D.W. Griffith and John Ford were early influential film directors. Since then, many of the world's most famous directors and actors have come from the U.S.

Fallingwater is one of Frank Lloyd Wright's most famous buildings.

American inventors have changed the world. Thomas Edison invented electric lighting and the phonograph. He also made improvements to the telegraph, telephone, and motion pictures.

Thomas Edison in his laboratory

The U.S. has made many contributions to the world. Its strength lies in its people, who enjoy the freedom and **democracy** guaranteed by its **Constitution**. Americans from all over the world are working to make the United States a great place to work and live.

Glossary

allies - countries that agree to help each other in times of need.

American Revolution - 1775 to 1783. A war for independence between Britain and its North American colonies. The colonists won and created the United States of America.

architecture - the art of planning and designing buildings. People who do this are called architects.

assassinate - to murder a very important person, usually for political reasons.

atomic bomb - a bomb that uses the energy of an atom. It is thousands of times more powerful than a regular bomb.

cease-fire - a suspension of hostile activities.

Civil War - a war between groups in the same country. The United States of America and the Confederate States of America fought a civil war from 1861 to 1865.

coniferous - a type of tree that bears needles or cones and does not lose its needles in the winter.

Constitution - the laws that govern the United States.

culture - the customs, arts, and tools of a nation or people at a certain time.

Declaration of Independence - an essay written at the Second Continental Congress in 1776, announcing the separation of the American colonies from England.

democracy - a governmental system in which the people vote on how to run the country.

Democrat - a member of the Democratic party. Democrats believe in social change and strong government.

economy - the way a nation uses its money, goods, and natural resources.

Great Depression - a period of economic hardship that started in 1929 and ended at the beginning of World War II.

hydroelectric - the kind of electricity produced by water-powered generators.

impeach - to have a trial to determine if a person should be removed from office.

Industrial Revolution - the period at the end of the nineteenth century during which the world economy was changed by the addition of new technology and machinery.

intermontane - the zone of cool, upland slopes below a timberline.

Korean War - 1950 to 1953. A war between North and South Korea. The American government sent troops to help South Korea.

migrate - to move from one place to settle in another.

New Deal - a group of programs designed to stimulate the economy during the Great Depression.

perjury - telling a lie when under oath to tell the truth.

Persian Gulf War - January 16, 1991, to February 28, 1991. A war in the Persian Gulf to liberate Kuwait from Iraqi forces.

petroleum - a thick, yellowish-black oil. It is the source of gasoline.

plateau - a raised area of flat land.

republic - a form of government in which authority rests with voting citizens and is carried out by elected officials.

Republican - a member of the Republican party. Republicans are conservative and believe in small government.

reservation - a piece of land set aside by the government for Native Americans to live on.

stock market - a place where stocks and bonds, which represent parts of businesses, are bought and sold.

terrorist - a person who uses violence to threaten people or governments.

Union - the states that remained in the U.S. during the Civil War.

Vietnam War - 1955 to 1975. A long, failed attempt by the U.S. to stop North Vietnam from taking over South Vietnam.

War on Terrorism - an international effort to keep the world safe from terrorist attacks.

World War I - 1914 to 1918, fought in Europe. The United States, Great Britain, France, Russia, and their allies were on one side. Germany, Austria-Hungary, and their allies were on the other side. The war began when Archduke Ferdinand of Austria was assassinated. The U.S. joined the war in 1917 because Germany began attacking ships that weren't involved in the war.

World War II - 1939 to 1945, fought in Europe, Asia, and Africa. The United States, France, Great Britain, the Soviet Union, and their allies were on one side. Germany, Italy, Japan, and their allies were on the other side. The war began when Germany invaded Poland. The U.S. entered the war in 1941, after Japan bombed Pearl Harbor, Hawaii.

Web Sites

Would you like to learn more about the United States? Please visit **www.abdopub.com** to find up-to-date Web site links about the country's government and people. These links are routinely monitored and updated to provide the most current information available.

Index